S0-ABA-591

WRITE ON CUE

BEGINNING ESL WRITING EXERCISES

To be used with
Cue Book 1, New Edition
The English for a Changing World Series
Imprint 1993 Copyright © 1984 by Glencoe/McGraw-Hill.
Copyright © 1984 Scott, Foresman and Company.
(ISBN 0-673-14547-6)

CHERYL KIRCHNER

GLENCOE
McGraw-Hill

New York, New York
Columbus, Ohio
Mission Hills, California
Peoria, Illinois

ISBN 0-673-24237-4

D'Nealian® Handwriting is a registered trademark of Donald N.
Thurber, licensed exclusively by Scott, Foresman and Company,
and is used here with permission.

Imprint 1995
Copyright © 1990 by Glencoe/McGraw-Hill. All rights reserved.
Copyright © 1990 Cheryl Kirchner. All rights reserved. Printed in
the United States of America.

Except as permitted under the United States Copyright Act, no
part of this publication may be reproduced or distributed in any
form or by any means, or stored in a database or retrieval system, without prior written permission from the publisher. Send
all inquiries to: Glencoe/McGraw-Hill, 936 Eastwind Drive,
Westerville, Ohio 43081.

5 6 7 8 9 10 11 12 13 14 15   QPK   02 01 00 99 98 97 96 95

ABOUT *WRITE ON CUE*

Write on Cue is a beginning writing book for the following adults and young adults:

- ESL (English as a Second Language) and EFL (English as a Foreign Language) students who have had limited academic training
- ESL/EFL students who need to be guided slowly and carefully through writing material in order for them to succeed
- ESL/EFL students who have no written native language or whose native language is not based on the Roman alphabet
- ABE (Adult Basic Education) students who need beginning writing practice at the word and simple-sentence levels

The deliberately slow and methodical presentation of material in this book is based upon three observations about adults and young adults who are beginning to write English: first, they are eager to start writing as part of their program of ESL study; second, they want, from the beginning, to write correctly; and, third, they are well aware of the gap between where they are in English and where they would like to be—proficient users of their new language.

Write on Cue is designed to encourage these students to write in spite of their limited English proficiency. The book offers "packages" of concrete, practical vocabulary with which to write; a carefully developed sequence of grammatical constructions to be mastered; and cue pictures to ensure that the process of writing will be interesting and will stimulate thinking. The material is broken into manageable segments so that students can experience the kind of success that in turn fosters the motivation to continue learning.

The exercises in *Write on Cue* are coodinated with the pictures in its companion booklet, the 1984 edition of *Cue Book 1* from the *English for a Changing World* series. However, it is *not* necessary to use the *English for a Changing World* student book in order to use *Write on Cue;* only *Cue Book 1* is needed. *Cue Book 1* organizes vocabulary around twenty practical, culturally oriented topics. *Write on Cue* and *Cue Book 1* form a writing package designed to cultivate good writing habits at the sentence level by interweaving vocabulary acquisition and grammar practice. *Write on Cue* systematically introduces and later reintegrates this content. Students infer their tasks through the use of models and then complete those tasks successfully.

Write on Cue can be used in multilevel writing classes or in open-entry/open-exit programs in which students work independently, proceeding through material at different rates. It can also be used in traditional classroom writing programs where teachers carefully control the preparatory activities, text assignments, and follow-up activities. The writing exercises in the book can be supplemented with oral/aural/reading activities. In short, *Write on Cue* can serve as a bridge to oral language skills, as a reinforcement of those skills, or as a skill-building tool in its own right.

The book consists of 160 exercises, including sixteen Checkup exercises. In addition, there are six Reading to Write units, each consisting of six activities. It's Your Cue questions appear frequently throughout the exercises to challenge students by giving them opportunities to personalize their responses. At the end of the book, instructors will find a Student Progress Chart. The chart is a blank form that can be reproduced as needed.

There are two kinds of numbering in the *Write on Cue* exercises:

- Item number followed by a period: 1.
  These numbers are strictly for the purpose of ordering the items in the exercises. They do *not* refer to numbered pictures in the *Cue Book 1* charts.
- Numbers in darker type printed in a grey box: **1**
  These numbers refer to numbered pictures in the *Cue Book 1* charts. Students need these references to complete almost all the writing exercises in *Write on Cue*.

For students who need more intensive practice in shape recognition, letters and numbers, and filling out forms, instructors may want to supplement the *Write on Cue* activities with others provided in the instructor's resource blackline master book, *Cuing In*. The *Cuing In* masters can be used before students begin *Write on Cue*; sections of the book can also be used directly with *Write on Cue*. In addition, the booklet *Cuing In with Pictures* is available for students who need an introduction to the *Write on Cue* system of using cue pictures as the basis for writing exercises. The writing tasks in *Cuing In with Pictures* are limited to copying vocabulary, recognizing vocabulary, and identifying vocabulary. The exercises are based on selected pictures from the *Cue Book 1* charts that are used in the beginning of *Write on Cue*. By completing *Cuing In with Pictures* before they go on to *Write on Cue*, students learn a procedure for mastering vocabulary. Students then use the vocabulary writing at the sentence level in *Write on Cue*.

I thank the following reviewers for sharing their ideas and opinions with me.

Christine Bunn: ESL Resource Instructor
Teacher Resource Center
San Francisco Community College Center
San Francisco, California

Rosemary Chavez: ESL Instructor
Milwaukee Area Technical College
Milwaukee, Wisconsin

Mona Kolacki: ESL Instructor
Bentley Adult Education Center
Livonia, Michigan

Mark Mankowski: ESL Instructor
Milwaukee Area Technical College
Milwaukee, Wisconsin

Tess Reinhard: ESL Consultant
Wonder Lake, Illinois

Gail Rice: Adult Basic Education Teacher
Palos Heights, Illinois

Claudia Rucinski: ESL Instructor
Milwaukee Area Technical College
Milwaukee, Wisconsin

I also thank Linda Rousos of Pima Community College, Tucson, Arizona, for her assistance on earlier versions of the manuscript. I am especially grateful to Mark Mankowski and Claudia Rucinski for their steadfast support of this project.

Finally, I dedicate this book to my family—especially Greg, Meagan, Travis, and Alexander—for their patience and encouragement.

GUIDE TO THE EXERCISES

WRITE ON CUE			CUE BOOK 1	
EXERCISE	**EXAMPLE**	**EXERCISE DESCRIPTION**	**CHART**	**TOPIC**
1	**1** tall _____tall_____	copying vocabulary	7	Adjectives
2	**7** hapy (happy)	recognizing correct spellings	7	Adjectives
3	**7** h a p p _y_	spelling correctly	7	Adjectives
4	**1** (the man) the woman	recognizing nouns	7	Adjectives
5	**13** _____the man_____	writing nouns	7	Adjectives
6	**/** (The man is tall.) / The man is tall	recognizing complete statements	7	Adjectives
7	**1** _____The man is tall._____	writing statements	7	Adjectives
8	**/** The man is tall. (He's tall.) She's tall. It's tall.	recognizing substitutions of pronouns for nouns in statements	7	Adjectives
9	**1** _____He's tall._____	writing statements	7	Adjectives
10	Mr (Mr.)	recognizing correct forms of titles	2	Names and Occupations
11	**1** _M r ._ Lane _Mr. Lane_	copying names	2	Names and Occupations
12	**1** bus driver _bus driver_	copying vocabulary	2	Names and Occupations
13	**/** bus driver _Mr._ Lane	writing titles	2	Names and Occupations
14	**1** (bus driver) bus drievr	recognizing correct spellings	2	Names and Occupations
15	**1** b u s d r i v _e_ _r_	spelling correctly	2	Names and Occupations

		WRITE ON CUE		CUE BOOK 1	
EXERCISE	**EXAMPLE**		**EXERCISE DESCRIPTION**	**CHART**	**TOPIC**
16	**1** _Mr. Lane is a bus driver._		writing statements	2	Names and Occupations
17	**/** Mr. Lane is a bus driver. _He_ _is_ a bus driver. _He's_ a bus driver.		writing pronouns as substitutions for nouns in statements	2	Names and Occupations
18	**1** _He's a bus driver._		writing statements	2	Names and Occupations
19	**1** book _book_		copying vocabulary	1	Classroom Objects
20	**1** (book) booke		recognizing correct spellings	1	Classroom Objects
21	**1** b _o_ _o_ k		spelling correctly	1	Classroom Objects
22	**/** It's a book (It's a book.)		recognizing complete statements	1	Classroom Objects
23	**1** _It's a book._		writing statements	1	Classroom Objects
24	**CHECKUP**			**1, 2, 7**	
25	**1** I am _I am_		copying the conjugation of _be_ in the present tense	5	Person and Number
26	I am ⟷ I'm **1** I'm I'am (I'm) Ia'm		recognizing the contracted forms of _be_ in the present tense	5	Person and Number
27	**1** I'm _I'm_		copying contractions of the conjugation of _be_ in the present tense	5	Person and Number

WRITE ON CUE			CUE BOOK 1	
EXERCISE	**EXAMPLE**	**EXERCISE DESCRIPTION**	**CHART**	**TOPIC**
28	**1** I'm (a student.) students.	recognizing the distinction between singular and plural nouns	5	Person and Number
29	**7** She's _a student_ .	writing nouns to complete statements	5	Person and Number
30	**7** (She's a student.) She's student.	recognizing complete statements	5	Person and Number
31	**1** _I'm a student._	writing statements	5	Person and Number
32	**CHECKUP**		**5**	
33	**1** accountant _accountant_	copying vocabulary	4	More Occupations
34	**1** acountant (accountant)	recognizing correct spellings	4	More Occupations
35	**1** a c c o u n t _a_ n t	spelling correctly	4	More Occupations
36	**/** She's a (an) accountant.	recognizing when to use *a* and *an*	4	More Occupations
37	**1** _an_ accountant	writing *a* or *an* with nouns	4	More Occupations
38	**1** He's a _She's an_ (She's) (an) _accountant._	writing statements	4	More Occupations
39	He's (a) _tall_ man. an **1** _He's a tall man._	writing statements with attributive adjectives	7	Adjectives
40	**CHECKUP**		**1, 2, 4, 7**	

WRITE ON CUE			CUE BOOK 1	
EXERCISE	**EXAMPLE**	**EXERCISE DESCRIPTION**	**CHART**	**TOPIC**
41	**2** (It's) / It isn't a chair. _It's a chair._	writing affirmative statements	1	Classroom Objects
42	**10** door _It isn't a door._ _It's a window._	writing affirmative and negative statements	1	Classroom Objects
43	**1** He's (He isn't) short. _He's tall._	writing affirmative statements	7	Adjectives
44	**1** short _He isn't short._ _He's tall._	writing affirmative and negative statements	7	Adjectives
45	**2** painter _He's a_ _painter._	writing affirmative and negative statements	4	More Occupations
46	**CHECKUP**		**1, 2, 4, 7**	
47	**/** (Is it) / It's a book?	recognizing the difference between statements and questions	1	Classroom Objects
48	**/** (Is it a book?) / Is it a book.	recognizing the difference between statements and questions	1	Classroom Objects
49	**/** Is it a book _?_	completing sentences with a question mark or a period	1	Classroom Objects
50	**1** _Is it a book?_	writing questions	1	Classroom Objects
51	**1** Is _she_ an accountant?	writing _he_ or _she_ and _a_ or _an_	4	More Occupations
52	**1** _Is he a bus driver?_	writing questions	2	Names and Occupations
53	**CHECKUP**		**1, 2, 4**	

WRITE ON CUE				CUE BOOK 1	
EXERCISE	**EXAMPLE**	**EXERCISE DESCRIPTION**		**CHART**	**TOPIC**
54	Is it a book? **1** (Yes, it is.) No, it isn't. It's _____ *a book* .	recognizing *Yes/No* short answers and completing statements		1	Classroom Objects
55	book _____ *Is it a book?* **9** _____ *No, it isn't. It's* _____ *a clock.*	writing questions and *Yes/No* short answers		1	Classroom Objects
56	**1** _____ *Is the man tall?* (he) she _____ *Yes, he is.* it	writing questions and *Yes* short answers		7	Adjectives
57	short _____ *Is the man short?* (he) **1** she _____ *No, he isn't.* it _____ *He's tall.*	writing questions and *No* short answers		7	Adjectives
58	**1** Is he a bus driver? *Yes, he is.*	writing *Yes/No* short answers		2	Names and Occupations
59	**CHECKUP**			**1, 2, 7**	
60	**1** _Who_ is _he_ ? *He's Mr. Lane.*	writing *Who* questions and answers		2	Names and Occupations
61	**1** _What_ is _he_ ? *He's a bus driver.*	writing *What* questions and answers		2	Names and Occupations
62	**1** Who (What) is he? He's a bus driver.	recognizing when to use *Who* and *What* in questions		2	Names and Occupations
63	**1** _Who_ is he? He's Mr. Lane. **1** What is he? He's _____ *a bus driver* .	writing *Who* or *What* in questions		2	Names and Occupations
64	**CHECKUP**			**2**	

WRITE ON CUE			CUE BOOK 1	
EXERCISE	EXAMPLE	EXERCISE DESCRIPTION	CHART	TOPIC
65	**1** **2** _Is it a book or a chair?_ **2** _It's a chair._	writing *or* questions and answers	1	Classroom Objects
66	**1** **2** _Is the man tall or short?_ **1** _He's tall._	writing *or* questions and answers	7	Adjectives
67	**1** red _red_	copying vocabulary	8	Colors
68	**1** read (red)	recognizing correct spellings	8	Colors
69	**1** r _e_ d	spelling correctly	8	Colors
70	**CHECKUP**		**8**	
71	**1** _The car is red._	writing statements with predicate adjectives	8	Colors
72	**1** _It's a red car._	writing statements with attributive adjectives	8	Colors
73	**13** _He's an angry man._	writing statements with attributive adjectives	7	Adjectives
74	_/_ Is the car red? _Is it a red car?_	writing questions with attributive or predicate adjectives	8	Colors
75	**1** Is the car red? _Yes, it is._	writing *Yes/No* short answers	8	Colors
76	**1** **2** _Is the car red or green?_ **2** _It's green._	writing *or* questions and answers	8	Colors
77	**CHECKUP**		**1, 7, 8**	
78	**3** tie _tie_	copying vocabulary	14	Clothes

WRITE ON CUE			CUE BOOK 1	
EXERCISE	**EXAMPLE**	**EXERCISE DESCRIPTION**	**CHART**	**TOPIC**
79	**3** ti (tie)	recognizing correct spellings	14	Clothes
80	**9** c _o_ _a_ t	spelling correctly	14	Clothes
81	**1** _shoes_ **3** _a tie_	writing singular and plural nouns	14	Clothes
82	**1** _What are they?_ _They're shoes._	writing *What* questions and answers about singular and plural nouns	14	Clothes
83	**7** He wearing pants. (He's wearing pants.)	recognizing complete statements	14	Clothes
84	**1** He _He's wearing shoes._	writing statements	14	Clothes
85	**2** hat _Is he wearing a hat?_ _Yes, he is._	writing questions and *Yes/No* short answers	7	Adjectives
86	**1** suit _a green suit_	writing the names of colors with singular and plural nouns	7	Adjectives
87	**1** (he) _What's he wearing?_ she hat _He's wearing a green hat._	writing *What* questions and answers	7	Adjectives
88	**10** red hat _She isn't_ _wearing a red hat._	writing affirmative and negative statements	2	Names and Occupations
89	**CHECKUP**		**2, 4**	
90	**1** behind _behind_	copying vocabulary	16	Prepositions of Location
91	**1** (behind) behin	recognizing correct spellings	16	Prepositions of Location
92	**1** b e h i _n_ _d_	spelling correctly	16	Prepositions of Location

WRITE ON CUE			CUE BOOK 1	
EXERCISE	EXAMPLE	EXERCISE DESCRIPTION	CHART	TOPIC
93	**1** The girl is _behind_ the car.	writing prepositions in statements	16	Prepositions of Location
94	**1** The girl _is_ behind the car.	writing *is* or *isn't*	16	Prepositions of Location
95	**1** behind _Is the girl behind the car?_ _Yes, she is._	writing questions and answers	16	Prepositions of Location
96	living room _living room_	copying vocabulary	11	Living Room and Bedroom
97	**1** (couch) coch	recognizing correct spellings	11	Living Room and Bedroom
98	**1** c o u _c_ _h_	spelling correctly	11	Living Room and Bedroom
99	Picture 1 is _a couch_ .	writing nouns with *a* and *an* in statements	11	Living Room and Bedroom
100	The radio is _on_ the table.	writing prepositions in statements	11	Living Room and Bedroom
101	bus _bus_ ; one _one_ ; 1 ⟷ one	copying vocabulary and matching numerals to spellings of numbers	6	Downtown Accident
102	Four chickens are _behind_ the waitress.	writing prepositions in statements	6	Downtown Accident
103	one chicken _on the_ _table_	charting facts	6	Downtown Accident
104	There is one chicken is in front of the truck. (There is one chicken in front) (of the truck.)	recognizing the correct forms of statements with *There is* and *There are*	6	Downtown Accident
105	(There is) _There is one_ There are _chicken on the table._	writing statements with *There is* and *There are*	6	Downtown Accident

WRITE ON CUE			CUE BOOK 1	
EXERCISE	**EXAMPLE**	**EXERCISE DESCRIPTION**	**CHART**	**TOPIC**
106	Are there five chickens on the truck? _No, there aren't. There are three chickens._	writing *Yes/No* answers using *There is* and *There are*	6	Downtown Accident
107	one there chicken is the mailbox in _There is one chicken in the mailbox._	writing words in the correct order to make a statement	6	Downtown Accident
108	**CHECKUP**		**6, 11, 14, 16**	
	READING TO WRITE 1	A. answering questions	10	The House
		B. writing the *-ing* forms of verbs		
		C. charting facts		
		D. writing **It's Your Cue** responses		
		E. writing words in the correct order to make statements		
		F. completing a cloze exercise		
109	**1** train station _train station_	copying vocabulary	3	The Community
110	**1** (train station) train statoin	recognizing correct spellings	3	The Community
111	**1** t r _a_ _i_ n s t a t _i_ _o_ n	spelling correctly	3	The Community
112	**1** at the _at the train station_	writing prepositional phrases using *at, on,* and *in*	3	The Community
113	_at_ the airport **2**	writing the prepositions *at, on,* and *in*	3	The Community

WRITE ON CUE			CUE BOOK 1	
EXERCISE	EXAMPLE	EXERCISE DESCRIPTION	CHART	TOPIC
114	**1** He _____ *He's at the train station.*	writing statements	3	The Community
115	**1** she _____ *Is she at the train station?*	writing questions	3	The Community
116	**CHECKUP**		**3**	
117	**1** hamburger *hamburger*	copying vocabulary	12	Food
118	**1** hambruger (hamburger)	recognizing correct spellings	12	Food
119	**1** h a m b <u>u</u> <u>r</u> g e r	spelling correctly	12	Food
120	**1** *a hamburger hamburgers* **3** *soup*	writing count and mass nouns	12	Food
121	**1** He _____ *He's eating a hamburger.*	writing statements with singular subject pronouns	12	Food
122	**1** He _____ *He's eating a hamburger.*	writing statements with singular and plural subject pronouns	12	Food
123	**7** pants shirt *He's wearing blue pants and a white shirt.*	writing statements with compound objects	4	More Occupations
	READING TO WRITE 2	A. answering questions	9	The Fair
		B. writing the *-ing* forms of verbs		
		C. charting facts		
		D. writing **It's Your Cue** responses		
		E. writing words in the correct order to make statements		

WRITE ON CUE			CUE BOOK 1	
EXERCISE	EXAMPLE	EXERCISE DESCRIPTION	CHART	TOPIC
		F. completing a cloze exercise		
124	**1** pear ___*pear*___	copying vocabulary	13	Fruits and Vegetables
125	**1** (pear) paer	recognizing correct spellings	13	Fruits and Vegetables
126	**1** p _e_ _a_ r	spelling correctly	13	Fruits and Vegetables
127	**1** ___*pear*___ ___*pears*___	writing count and mass nouns	13	Fruits and Vegetables
128	**1** he ___*Is he buying pears?*___	writing questions	13	Fruits and Vegetables
129	**1** ___*I want*___	copying the conjugation of *want* in the present tense	5	Person and Number
130	**12** **14** He ___*He wants some green beans and lettuce.*___	writing statements including *some . . . and* combinations	13	Fruits and Vegetables
131	**1** ___*I don't want*___	copying the forms of the negative conjugation of *want* in the simple present tense	5	Person and Number
132	**11** **14** He ___*He doesn't want any cherries or lettuce.*___	writing statements including *any . . . or* combinations	13	Fruits and Vegetables
133	**/** We want ___*some*___ pears.	writing *some* and *any*	13	Fruits and Vegetables

WRITE ON CUE			CUE BOOK 1	
EXERCISE	**EXAMPLE**	**EXERCISE DESCRIPTION**	**CHART**	**TOPIC**
134	☐ *1* ☐ *16* We want (some pears and apples.) any pears or apples.	recognizing when to use *some . . . and* and *any . . . or*	13	Fruits and Vegetables
135	**4** **8** I (NEGATIVE) *I don't want any salad or fish.*	writing *some . . . and* and *any . . . or* statements	12	Food
136	**CHECKUP**		**12, 13**	
	READING TO WRITE 3	A. answering questions	15	The Party
		B. writing the *-ing* forms of verbs		
		C. charting facts		
		D. writing **It's Your Cue** responses		
		E. writing words in the correct order to make statements		
		F. completing a cloze exercise		
137	**1** play soccer *play soccer*	copying vocabulary	17	Games
138	**1** play socer (play soccer)	recognizing correct spellings	17	Games
139	**5** p l a y c h _e_ s s	spelling correctly	17	Games
140	**1** *play soccer* **12** *sail*	writing verbs	17	Games
141	**1** he *Does he play soccer?*	writing questions	17	Games
142	☐ *1* Does he play soccer? Yes *Yes, he does.*	writing *Yes/No* short answers	17	Games

WRITE ON CUE				CUE BOOK 1	
EXERCISE	EXAMPLE		EXERCISE DESCRIPTION	CHART	TOPIC
143	**1** _Does_ she want a hamburger? Yes, she _wants_ a hamburger.		writing verbs forms in questions and answers	12	Food
144	**1** you _How many hamburgers do you want?_		writing questions with *How much* and *How many*	12	Food
145	**1** you _How many pears do you want?_ (AFFIRMATIVE) _I want a lot of pears._		writing questions with *How much* and *How many* and affirmative and negative answers	13	Fruits and Vegetables
146	**CHECKUP**			**12, 13, 17**	
	READING TO WRITE 4		A. answering questions	18	Outside the Hotel
			B. writing the *-ing* forms of verbs		
			C. charting facts		
			D. writing **It's Your Cue** responses		
			E. writing words in the correct order to make statements		
			F. completing a cloze exercise		
147	**1** I _I'm buying some pears._ **2** _I want to buy some peaches too._		writing statements	13	Fruits and Vegetables
148	**2** she _Does she want to buy some socks?_ No _No, she doesn't._		writing questions and *Yes/No* short answers	14	Clothes

	WRITE ON CUE			CUE BOOK 1	
EXERCISE	EXAMPLE	EXERCISE DESCRIPTION	CHART	TOPIC	
149	*1* _Do_ you want to buy some pears? No, I _don't_ want to buy any pears.	writing verb forms in questions and answers	13	Fruits and Vegetables	
150	**1** He _He likes to play soccer._	writing statements	17	Games	
151	**1** He _He doesn't like to play soccer._	writing negative statements	17	Games	
152	**1** he _Does he like to play soccer?_	writing questions	17	Games	
153	**CHECKUP**		**17**		
	READING TO WRITE 5	A. answering questions	19	The Seasons	
		B. writing the *-ing* forms of verbs			
		C. charting facts			
		D. writing **It's Your Cue** responses			
		E. writing words in the correct order to make statements			
		F. completing a cloze exercise			
154	**1** My _My_	copying and identifying possessive pronouns	5	Person and Number	
155	**1** I _have_ a doctor. _My_ doctor is old.	writing *have* and *has* and possessive pronouns	5	Person and Number	
156	**1** me _me_	copying and identifying object pronouns	5	Person and Number	

EXERCISE	EXAMPLE	EXERCISE DESCRIPTION	CHART	TOPIC
157	Mr. Lane has a telephone. (He) She has a telephone. It's (his) her telephone number. Call (him.) her.	recognizing when to use subject, possessive, and object pronouns	5	Person and Number
158	**1** _I_ have a telephone. It's _my_ telephone number. Call _me._	writing subject, possessive, and object pronouns	5	Person and Number
159	**4** hot dogs _Give them some hot dogs, please._	writing statements	5	Person and Number
160	**CHECKUP**		**4, 5**	
	READING TO WRITE 6	A. answering questions	20	In the Hotel
		B. writing the *-ing* forms of verbs		
		C. charting facts		
		D. writing **It's Your Cue** responses		
		E. writing words in the correct order to make statements		
		F. completing a cloze exercise		

Chart 7 | **EXERCISE 1**

Copy.

1 tall

t a l l

tall

tall

2 short

s h o r t

short

short

3 big

— — —

————

————

5 ugly

— — — —

————

————

7 happy

— — — — —

————

————

1 tall

— — — — —

————

————

2 short

— — — — — —

————

————

4 little

— — — — — —

————

————

6 beautiful

— — — — — — — —

————

————

8 sad

— — —

————

————

→

9 thin

_ _ _ _

_____

_____

10 fat

_ _ _

_____

_____

11 young

_ _ _ _ _

_____

_____

12 old

_ _ _

_____

_____

13 angry

_ _ _ _ _

_____

_____

14 thirsty

_ _ _ _ _ _ _

_____

_____

15 hungry

_ _ _ _ _ _

_____

_____

16 tired

_ _ _ _ _

_____

_____

17 new

_ _ _

_____

_____

18 old

_ _ _

_____

_____

Chart 7 | **EXERCISE 2**

Circle the correct spelling.

1. **7** hapy ⟨happy⟩   2. **9** ⟨thin⟩ then

3. **17** nuw new   4. **1** tal tall

5. **4** litle little   6. **14** thirsty thristy

7. **3** gib big   8. **16** tried tired

9. **8** sad das   10. **12** **18** od old

11. **2** short shrot   12. **13** anrgy angry

13. **6** beutiful beautiful   14. **10** taf fat

15. **15** hungry hunrgy   16. **11** yung young

17. **5** ulgy ugly   18. **7** hapy happy

19. **9** thin then

Chart 7 | **EXERCISE 3**

Write the letters.

1. **7** happ *y*   2. **10** f _a_ t

3. **17** ne _   4. **2** _ _ ort

5. **3** b _ g   6. **12** **18** o _ d

7. **9** _ _ in   8. **1** t _ ll

9. **15** h _ ngry   10. **8** sa _

11. **5** u _ _ y   12. **16** tir _ _

13. **6** be _ _ tiful   14. **14** thi _ _ ty

15. **4** litt _ _   16. **11** you _ _

17. **13** an _ _ y

Chart 7 | **EXERCISE 4**

	the man	the boy	the dog
the	the woman	the girl	the car

Circle the correct words.

1. **1** (the man) the woman
2. **1** the man the woman
3. **3** the car (the dog)
4. **3** the car the dog
5. **5** the boy the girl
6. **8** the woman the man
7. **9** the man the woman
8. **11** the boy the girl
9. **12** the woman the man
10. **13** the man the woman
11. **14** the woman the boy
12. **15** the man the girl
13. **16** the woman the man
14. **18** the car the dog

Chart 7 | **EXERCISE 5**

Copy.

the man

t h e   m a n

the man

the man

the woman

_ _ _   _ _ _ _ _

_____

_____

the man

_ _ _   _ _ _

_____

_____

the boy

_ _ _   _ _ _

_____

_____

| Chart 7 | **EXERCISE 8** |

	LONG FORMS		CONTRACTIONS
The man is The boy is	}	He is →	He's
The woman is The girl is	}	She is →	She's
The dog is The car is	}	It is →	It's

APOSTROPHE	'

Write the picture number. Then circle the correct statement.

1. | 1 | The man is tall.

(He's tall.)
She's tall.
It's tall.

2. | 5 | The girl is ugly.

He's ugly.
(She's ugly.)
It's ugly.

3. | 18 | The car is old.

He's old.
She's old.
(It's old.)

4. | | The man is short.

He's short.
She's short.
It's short.

5. | | The boy is young.

He's young.
She's young.
It's young.

→

6. [ ] The man is angry.

He's angry.
She's angry.
It's angry.

7. [ ] The woman is fat.

He's fat.
She's fat.
It's fat.

8. [ ] The man is happy.

He's happy.
She's happy.
It's happy.

9. [ ] The dog is little.

He's little.
She's little.
It's little.

10. [ ] The man is tired.

He's tired.
She's tired.
It's tired.

11. [ ] The man is old.

He's old.
She's old.
It's old.

12. [ ] The car is new.

He's new.
She's new.
It's new.

13. [ ] The girl is beautiful.

He's beautiful.
She's beautiful.
It's beautiful.

14. [ ] The woman is thin.

He's thin.
She's thin.
It's thin.

15. ☐ The dog is big.

He's big.

She's big.

It's big.

16. ☐ The man is sad.

He's sad.

She's sad.

It's sad.

17. ☐ The woman is thirsty.

He's thirsty.

She's thirsty.

It's thirsty.

| Chart 7 | **EXERCISE 9**

Copy.

He's   He's   She's   It's

H e ' s   _ _ _ _ _   _ _ _ _ _ _   _ _ _ _

He's   _____   _____   _____

He's   _____   _____   _____

Write the statement.

1. **1** *He's tall.* _____

2. **9** *She's thin.* _____

3. **4** *It's little.* _____

4. **5** _____

5. **18** _____

6. **8** _____

7. **15** _____

→

8. **2** _____

9. **12** _____

10. **16** _____

11. **13** _____

12. **17** _____

13. **11** _____

14. **6** _____

15. **14** _____

16. **3** _____

17. **10** _____

18. **7** _____

19. **4** _____

20. **1** _____

21. **9** _____

It's Your Cue

Look at Chart 7. Write four statements about your teacher. Use He's or She's.

_____

_____

_____

_____

15 doctor

_ _ _ _ _ _

_____

_____

Chart 2 | **EXERCISE 13**

Write the picture number and the title if necessary.

1. ☐ *1*   bus driver   ____*Mr.*____ Lane

2. ☐ *12*   cashier   ____*Mrs.*____ Silver

3. ☐   policeman   _____ Brown

4. ☐   carpenter   _____ Wood

5. ☐   photographer   _____ Lens

6. ☐   waiter   _____ Glass

7. ☐   waitress   _____ Butler

8. ☐   teacher   _____ Brown

9. ☐   mechanic   _____ Phillips

10. ☐   saleswoman   _____ Sellers

11. ☐   reporter   _____ Bell

12. ☐   mailman   _____ Post

13. ☐   student   Tina

14. ☐   student   Dick

15. ☐   doctor   _____ White

16. ☐   cashier   _____ Silver

17. ☐   bus driver   _____ Lane

Chart 2   **EXERCISE 14**

Circle the correct spelling.

1. **1** (bus driver)   bus drievr
2. **5** waitres   (waitress)
3. **11** **13** stuednt   student
4. **6** mecanic   mechanic
5. **14** teachr   teacher
6. **2** saleswoman   saelswoman
7. **8** photograper   photographer
8. **9** water   waiter
9. **3** carpenter   carpnter
10. **15** doctor   docter
11. **7** policman   policeman
12. **10** reproter   reporter
13. **4** mailman   maiman
14. **12** casher   cashier
15. **5** waitres   waitress
16. **1** bus driver   bus drievr

Chart 2   **EXERCISE 15**

Write the letters.

1. **1** bus driv _e_ _r_   2. **7** poli _c_ _e_ man
3. **8** photogra __ __ er   4. **9** w __ __ ter

5. **11** **13** studen __   6. **3** carpent __ __

7. **4** m __ __ lman   8. **6** me __ __ anic

9. **10** report __ __   10. **2** sal __ __ woman

11. **5** w __ __ tress   12. **14** t __ __ cher

13. **12** cash __ __ r   14. **15** doct __ __

15. **7** poli __ __ man   16. **1** bus driv __ __

Chart 2 | **EXERCISE 16**

| is | | a |

Write the statement.

1. **1** *Mr. Lane is a bus driver.* _____

2. **1** _____

3. **2** *Mrs. Sellers is a saleswoman.* _____

4. **2** _____

5. **3** _____

6. **4** _____

7. **5** _____

8. **6** _____

9. **7** _____

10. **8** _____

11. **9** _____

12. **10** _____

$\longrightarrow$

13. **11** _____

14. **12** _____

15. **13** _____

16. **14** _____

17. **15** _____

| Chart 2 | **EXERCISE 17** |

LONG FORMS   CONTRACTIONS

Mr. Lane is ⎫
            ⎬ He is   ⟶   He's
Dick is   ⎭

Mrs. Sellers is ⎫
Miss Butler is ⎬ She is   ⟶   She's
Tina is   ⎭

Write the picture number. Then write the correct words.

He is   She is
He's   She's

1. **/** Mr. Lane is a bus driver.

    _He_ _is_ a bus driver.

    _He's_ a bus driver.

2. **12** Mrs. Silver is a cashier.

    She _is_ a cashier.

    She's a cashier.

3. ☐ Mr. Phillips is a mechanic.

   _____ _____ a mechanic.

   _____ a mechanic.

4. ☐ Mr. Wood is a carpenter.

   _____ _____ a carpenter.

   _____ a carpenter.

5. ☐ Mr. Post is a mailman.

   _____ _____ a mailman.

   _____ a mailman.

6. ☐ Dr. White is a doctor.

   _____ _____ a doctor.

   _____ a doctor.

7. ☐ Mr. Glass is a waiter.

   _____ _____ a waiter.

   _____ a waiter.

8. ☐ Mrs. Sellers is a saleswoman.

   _____ _____ a saleswoman.

   _____ a saleswoman.

9. ☐ Miss Bell is a reporter.

   _____ _____ a reporter.

   _____ a reporter.

10. ☐ Mrs. Brown is a teacher.

   _____ _____ a teacher.

   _____ a teacher.

→

11. ☐ Dick is a student.

_____ _____ a student.

_____ a student.

12. ☐ Mr. Brown is a policeman.

_____ _____ a policeman.

_____ a policeman.

13. ☐ Tina is a student.

_____ _____ a student.

_____ a student.

14. ☐ Miss Lens is a photographer.

_____ _____ a photographer.

_____ a photographer.

15. ☐ Miss Butler is a waitress.

_____ _____ a waitress.

_____ a waitress.

Chart 2 | **EXERCISE 18**

He's   She's

Write the statement.

1. **1**   *He's a bus driver.* _____

2. **2**   *She's a saleswoman.* _____

3. **11** _____

4. **5** _____

5. **13** _____

6. **4** _____

7. **8** _____

8. **3** _____

9. **14** _____

10. **15** _____

11. **7** _____

12. **12** _____

13. **9** _____

14. **6** _____

15. **10** _____

It's Your Cue

Look at Chart 2. Write about the occupations of three of your classmates. Use He's *or* She's.

_____

_____

_____

Chart 1 | **EXERCISE 19**

Copy.

1 book

b o o k

book

book

1 book

— — — —

————

————

2 chair

— — — — —

————

————

3 calendar

— — — — — — — —

————

————

4 table

— — — — —

————

————

5 door

— — — —

————

————

6 desk

— — — —

————

————

7 pen

— — —

————

————

8 blackboard

— — — — — — — — —

————

————

9 clock

— — — — —

————

————

10 window

_ _ _ _ _ _

_____

_____

11 pencil

_ _ _ _ _ _

_____

_____

12 chalk

_ _ _ _ _

_____

_____

13 eraser

_ _ _ _ _ _

_____

_____

14 wastebasket

_ _ _ _ _ _ _ _ _ _

_____

_____

15 ruler

_ _ _ _ _

_____

_____

| Chart 1 | **EXERCISE 20** |

Circle the correct spelling.

1. **1** (book) booke
2. **8** blakboard (blackboard)
3. **14** wastbasket wastebasket
4. **10** windo window
5. **5** door dor
6. **9** clock clok
7. **3** caledar calendar
8. **2** chiar chair
9. **15** ruler ruelr
10. **11** pencl pencil
11. **12** chak chalk
12. **6** desk deks
13. **7** pen nep
14. **13** eraser erasr
15. **4** tabel table

Chart 1 | **EXERCISE 21**

Write the letters.

1. **1** b o o k
2. **4** tab l e
3. **12** cha _ _
4. **15** r _ ler
5. **9** clo _ _
6. **7** p _ n
7. **3** calend _ r
8. **14** wasteba _ _ et
9. **5** d _ _ r
10. **2** _ _ air
11. **11** pen _ _ l
12. **8** blackb _ _ rd
13. **13** era _ er
14. **10** w _ nd _ _
15. **6** de _ _

Chart 1 | **EXERCISE 22**

It is
↓ ↓
It's

CAPITAL
LETTER   PERIOD
↓   ↓
It's a book.

It's a chair.

Write the picture number. Then circle the correct statement.

1. **1**   It's a book
   (It's a book.)

2. **8**   it's a blackboard.
   (It's a blackboard.)

3. _____ It's an eraser.
   It's an eraser

4. _____ it's a clock.
   It's a clock.

5. ☐ It's a desk.
   it's a desk.

6. ☐ It's a calendar.
   It's a calendar

7. ☐ it's a pencil.
   It's a pencil.

8. ☐ It's a door
   It's a door.

9. ☐ it's a ruler.
   It's a ruler.

10. ☐ It's a pen.
    it's a pen.

11. ☐ It's chalk
    It's chalk.

12. ☐ It's a table.
    it's a table.

13. ☐ It's a wastebasket.
    It's a wastebasket

14. ☐ it's a chair.
    It's a chair.

15. ☐ It's a window.
    It's a window

| Chart 1 | **EXERCISE 23** |

| It is |
| \ / |
| It's | | a |

Write the statement.

1. **1** _It's a book._

2. **5** _It's a door._

3. **9** _____

4. **10** _____

→

5. **7** _____

6. **2** _____

7. **14** _____

8. **8** _____

9. **4** _____

10. **6** _____

11. **11** _____

12. **3** _____

13. **15** _____

14. **5** _____

15. **1** _____

16. **12** It's chalk.

17. **13** It's an eraser.

EXERCISE 24

Write the statement. Use He's, She's, *or* It's.

Chart 1

1. **1**   *It's a book.*
2. **6**   _____
3. **9**   _____
4. **7**   _____

Chart 2

5. **2**   _____
6. **15** _____
7. **6**   _____
8. **4**   _____
9. **5**   _____

Chart 7

10. **12** *He's old.*
11. **14** _____
12. **3** _____
13. **17** _____
14. **11** _____
15. **9** _____
16. **18** _____

Chart 5 | **EXERCISE 25**

SINGULAR	PLURAL
I am	we are
you are	you are
he is	
	they are
she is	

Copy.

SINGULAR

1 I am

I   a m

I am

1 I am

— ——

————

2 you are

——— ———

————

3 he is

—— ——

————

7 she is

——— ——

————

PLURAL

5 we are

we   a r e

we are

5 we are

—— ———

————

6 you are

——— ———

————

4 they are

———— ———

————

| Chart 5 | **EXERCISE 26** |

Match the long form with the contraction.

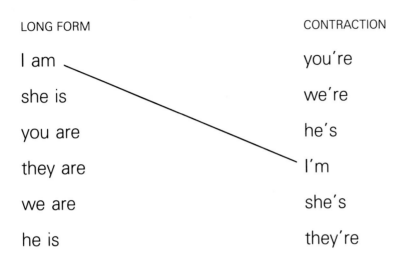

LONG FORM	CONTRACTION
I am	you're
she is	we're
you are	he's
they are	I'm
we are	she's
he is	they're

Circle the word that is the same.

1.	**1**	I'm	I'am	(I'm)	Ia'm
2.	**5**	we're	w'ere	we'are	(we're)
3.	**3**	he's	h'es	he's	he'is
4.	**2** **6**	you're	yo're	your'e	you're
5.	**4**	they're	they're	the'yre	theyr'e
6.	**7**	she's	sh'es	she'is	she's
7.	**5**	we're	w'ere	we'are	we're
8.	**1**	I'm	I'am	I'm	Ia'm

Chart 5 | **EXERCISE 27**

Copy.

SINGULAR

1 I'm

I ' m

I'm

I'm

1 I'm

— — —

_____

_____

2 you're

— — — — — —

_____

_____

3 he's

— — — —

_____

_____

7 she's

— — — — —

_____

_____

PLURAL

5 we're

w e ' r e

we're

we're

5 we're

— — — — —

_____

_____

6 you're

— — — — — —

_____

_____

4 they're

— — — — — — —

_____

_____

Chart 7 | **EXERCISE 43**

AFFIRMATIVE	NEGATIVE
He's	He isn't
She's	She isn't
It's	It isn't

Circle the correct words. Then write the affirmative statement.

1. **1** He's
   (He isn't) short.

   He's tall.

2. **15** (He's)
   He isn't hungry.

   He's hungry.

3. **9** She's
   She isn't fat.

   _____

4. **7** He's
   He isn't sad.

   _____

5. **12** He's
   He isn't old.

   _____

$\longrightarrow$

6. **2** He's
He isn't short.

_____

7. **6** She's
She isn't ugly.

_____

8. **14** She's
She isn't thirsty.

_____

9. **17** It's
It isn't new.

_____

10. **3** It's
It isn't little.

_____

11. **15** He's
He isn't angry.

_____

12. **18** It's
It isn't new.

_____

13. **16** He's
He isn't tired.

_____

14. **2** He's
He isn't tall.

_____

Chart 7 | **EXERCISE 44**

AFFIRMATIVE	NEGATIVE
He's	He isn't
She's	She isn't
It's	It isn't

Write the statements.

1. **1** short *He isn't short.*

He's tall.

2. **15** hungry *He's hungry.*

3. **7** happy _____

4. **17** old _____

_____

5. **4** angry _____

_____

6. **14** tired _____

_____

7. **10** fat _____

$\longrightarrow$

8. **3** little _____

_____

9. **18** new _____

_____

10. **8** sad _____
11. **16** big _____

_____

12. **6** beautiful _____
13. **13** hungry _____

_____

14. **9** thirsty _____

_____

15. **12** young _____

_____

16. **5** fat _____

_____

17. **2** short _____
18. **11** young _____
19. **15** hungry _____
20. **1** short _____

_____

Chart 4 | **EXERCISE 45**

	AFFIRMATIVE	NEGATIVE
	He's	He isn't
	She's	She isn't
	It's	It isn't

a
an

Write the statements.

1. [2] painter *He's a painter.* _____

2. [10] lawyer *She isn't a lawyer.* _____

   She's a nurse. _____

3. [4] optician _____

4. [8] doctor _____

   _____

5. [7] engineer _____

   _____

6. [1] nurse _____

   _____

7. [3] architect _____

8. [9] dentist _____

9. [5] accountant _____

   _____

10. [6] secretary _____

   _____

EXERCISE 46

Write the correct words. He's She's It's
 He isn't She isn't It isn't

Chart 1 1. **11** *It's* _____ a pencil.

 2. **6** *It isn't* _____ a table.

 3. **15** _____ an eraser.

 4. **9** _____ a clock.

Chart 2 5. **6** _____ a mechanic.

 6. **13** _____ a waitress.

 7. **2** _____ a saleswoman.

 8. **3** _____ a carpenter.

Chart 4 9. **3** _____ a workman.

 10. **5** _____ an optician.

 11. **9** _____ a dentist.

 12. **6** _____ an engineer.

Chart 7 13. **16** _____ angry.

 14. **4** _____ little.

 15. **8** _____ happy.

 16. **12** _____ old.

 17. **10** _____ thin.

 18. **1** _____ short.

Chart 1 | **EXERCISE 47**

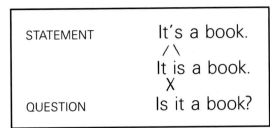

STATEMENT	It's a book.
	/ \
	It is a book.
	X
QUESTION	Is it a book?

PERIOD	.
QUESTION MARK	?

Write the picture number. Then circle the correct words.

1. | 1 | (Is it) / It's | a book?

2. | 4 | Is it / (It's) | a table.

3. | | It's / Is it | a pen?

4. | | It is / Is it | a clock.

5. | | It's / Is it | a chair.

6. | | Is it / It's | chalk?

7. | | It's / Is it | an eraser.

8. | | Is it / It is | a wastebasket.

9. | | It's / Is it | a ruler?

10. | | It is / Is it | a desk?

11. | | It is / Is it | a calendar.

12. | | It's / Is it | a blackboard?

13. | | Is it / It is | a pencil.

14. | | Is it / It's | a door.

15. | | It's / Is it | a window?

16. | | Is it / It's | a book?

17. | | Is it / It's | a table.

Chart 1 | **EXERCISE 48**

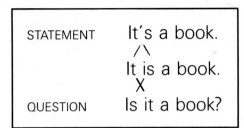

STATEMENT	It's a book.
	/\
	It is a book.
	X
QUESTION	Is it a book?

Write the picture number. Then circle the correct statement or question.

1. 『 / 』 (Is it a book?)
   Is it a book.

2. 『 9 』 it's a clock.
   (It's a clock.)

3. 『 』 Is it a chair?
   Is it a chair

4. 『 』 is it a door?
   Is it a door?

5. 『 』 It's a blackboard.
   it is a blackboard.

6. 『 』 It is a window.
   It is a window

7. 『 』 is it a table?
   Is it a table?

8. 『 』 It's a calendar
   Is it a calendar?

9. 『 』 Is it a ruler
   Is it a ruler?

10. 『 』 It's a wastebasket.
    Is it a wastebasket.

11. 『 』 it's a pencil.
    It is a pencil.

12. 『 』 Is it a desk.
    Is it a desk?

13. 『 』 It is a pen.
    it's a pen.

14. 『 』 It's an eraser.
    It is an eraser

15. 『 』 it is chalk.
    Is it chalk?

16. 『 』 Is it a book?
    Is it a book.

17. 『 』 it's a clock.
    It's a clock.

Chart 1 | **EXERCISE 49**

STATEMENT	It's a book.
	/\
	It is a book.
	X
QUESTION	Is it a book?

PERIOD	.
QUESTION MARK	?

Copy.

QUESTION MARK   ?

—

—

—

Write the picture number. Then write the period or question mark.   .   ?

1. [/] Is it a book ?

2. [/] It's a book __

3. [ ] It is a book __

4. [ ] Is it a clock __

5. [ ] It's a blackboard __

6. [ ] Is it a pencil __

7. [ ] It is a chair __

8. [ ] Is it chalk __

9. [ ] It's a table __

10. [ ] It is a desk __

11. [ ] Is it a wastebasket __

12. [ ] It's a pen __

13. [ ] Is it a door __

14. [ ] Is it a window __

15. [ ] It's a calendar __

16. [ ] Is it a ruler __

17. [ ] It is an eraser __

18. [ ] It's a book __

19. [ ] It is a book __

20. [ ] Is it a book __

| Chart 1 | **EXERCISE 50** |

QUESTION   Is it a book?

a
an

Write the question.

1. **1**   *Is it a book?*

2. **10**   *Is it a window?*

3. **2**   _____

4. **6**   _____

5. **9**   _____

6. **14**   _____

7. **4**   _____

8. **7**   _____

9. **13**   _____

10. **3**   _____

11. **5**   _____

12. **15**   _____

13. **8**   _____

14. **11**   _____

15. **10**   _____

16. **1**   _____

17. **12**   Is it chalk?

Chart 4 | **EXERCISE 51**

STATEMENT	He's a painter.	She's an accountant.
	/\	/\
	He is a painter.	She is an accountant.
	X	✕
QUESTION	Is he a painter?	Is she an accountant?

Write the correct word.   he   she   a   an

1. **1**   Is _she_ an accountant?

2. **2**   Is he _a_ painter?

3. **9**   Is she _____ dentist?

4. **4**   Is she _____ optician?

5. **7**   Is _____ a workman?

6. **6**   Is he _____ engineer?

7. **3**   Is _____ an architect?

8. **10** Is _____ a nurse?

9. **8**   Is she _____ secretary?

10. **5**   Is _____ a lawyer?

11. **2**   Is he _____ painter?

12. **1**   Is _____ an accountant?

Chart 2 | **EXERCISE 52**

STATEMENT	He's a bus driver. She's a saleswoman.
	He is a bus driver. She is a saleswoman.
QUESTION	Is he a bus driver? Is she a saleswoman?

Write the question.

1. **1**   *Is he a bus driver?* _____

2. **2**   *Is she a saleswoman?* _____

3. **9**   _____

4. **4**   _____

5. **6**   _____

6. **10**   _____

7. **13**   _____

8. **5**   _____

9. **3**   _____

10. **8**   _____

11. **11**   _____

12. **15**   _____

13. **7**   _____

14. **12**   _____

15. **14**   _____

Chart 2 | **EXERCISE 60**

> Who is he?   He's Mr. Lane.
>
> Who is she?   She's Mrs. Sellers.

Write the correct words in the question. Who   he   she
Then write the answer.

1. **1** ___Who___ is ___he___ ? _He's Mr. Lane._____
2. **1** _____ is _____ ? _____
3. **2** ___Who___ is ___she___ ? _She's Mrs. Sellers.___
4. **2** _____ is _____ ? _____
5. **3** _____ is _____ ? _____
6. **4** _____ is _____ ? _____
7. **5** _____ is _____ ? _____
8. **6** _____ is _____ ? _____
9. **7** _____ is _____ ? _____
10. **8** _____ is _____ ? _____
11. **9** _____ is _____ ? _____
12. **10** _____ is _____ ? _____
13. **11** _____ is _____ ? _____
14. **12** _____ is _____ ? _____
15. **13** _____ is _____ ? _____
16. **14** _____ is _____ ? _____
17. **15** _____ is _____ ? _____

| Chart 2 | **EXERCISE 61** |

> What is he?   He's a bus driver.
>
> What is she?   She's a saleswoman.

Write the correct words in the question.   What   he   she
Then write the answer.

1. | **1** | ___*What*___ is ___*he*___ ? ___*He's a bus driver.*___

2. | **1** | _____ is _____ ? _____

3. | **2** | ___*What*___ is ___*she*___ ? ___*She's a saleswoman.*___

4. | **2** | _____ is _____ ? _____

5. | **3** | _____ is _____ ? _____

6. | **4** | _____ is _____ ? _____

7. | **5** | _____ is _____ ? _____

8. | **6** | _____ is _____ ? _____

9. | **7** | _____ is _____ ? _____

10. | **8** | _____ is _____ ? _____

11. | **9** | _____ is _____ ? _____

12. | **10** | _____ is _____ ? _____

13. | **11** | _____ is _____ ? _____

14. | **12** | _____ is _____ ? _____

15. | **13** | _____ is _____ ? _____

16. | **14** | _____ is _____ ? _____

17. | **15** | _____ is _____ ? _____

Chart 2 **EXERCISE 62**

Who is he?   He's Mr. Lane.

What is he?   He's a bus driver.

Who is she?   She's Mrs. Sellers.

What is she?   She's a saleswoman.

Circle Who *or* What.

1. **1** Who
   (What) is he?   He's a bus driver.

2. **1** Who
   What is he?   He's a bus driver.

3. **2** (Who)
   What is she?   She's Mrs. Sellers.

4. **2** Who
   What is she?   She's Mrs. Sellers.

5. **3** Who
   What is he?   He's a carpenter.

6. **4** Who
   What is he?   He's Mr. Post.

7. **5** Who
   What is she?   She's Miss Butler.

8. **6** Who
   What is he?   He's a mechanic.

$\longrightarrow$

9. **7** Who / What is he? He's Mr. Brown.

10. **8** Who / What is she? She's Miss Lens.

11. **9** Who / What is he? He's a waiter.

12. **10** Who / What is she? She's a reporter.

13. **11** Who / What is he? He's a student.

14. **12** Who / What is she? She's a cashier.

15. **13** Who / What is she? She's Tina.

16. **14** Who / What is she? She's Mrs. Brown.

17. **15** Who / What is he? He's a doctor.

Chart 8 | **EXERCISE 71**

Write the statement.

1. **1** _The car is red._
2. **8** _____
3. **5** _____
4. **10** _____
5. **2** _____
6. **9** _____
7. **4** _____
8. **6** _____
9. **7** _____

Chart 8 | **EXERCISE 72**

The car is   red.
↓ ✓   ↓
It's   a red car.

a
an

Write the statement. Use It's.

1. **1** _It's a red car._
2. **7** _____
3. **11** _____
4. **3** _____

→

5. **6** _____

6. **2** _____

7. **5** _____

8. **9** _____

9. **4** _____

| Chart 7 | **EXERCISE 73** |

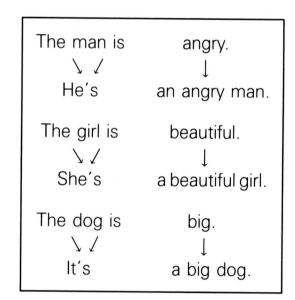

Write the statement. Use He's, She's, *or* It's.

1. **13** *He's an angry man.* _____

2. **6** *She's a beautiful girl.* _____

3. **3** *It's a big dog.* _____

4. **10** _____

5. **2** _____

6. **14** _____

7. **16** _____

8. **5** _____

9. **9** _____

10. **11** _____

11. **18** _____

12. **17** _____

13. **4** _____

14. **1** _____

15. **12** _____

Chart 8	**EXERCISE 74**

```
Is      the car        red?

                ↓            ↓

Is      it        a red car?
```

a
an

Write the picture number. Then write the question.

1. **/** Is the car red? *Is it a red car?* _____

2. **☐** Is the car blue? _____

3. **☐** Is the car orange? _____

4. **☐** Is the car green? _____

5. **☐** Is the car purple? _____

6. **☐** Is the car yellow? _____

→

7. [ ] Is the car red? _____

8. [7] *Is the car black?* _____ Is it a black car?

9. [ ] _____ Is it a brown car?

10. [ ] _____ Is it a pink car?

11. [ ] _____ Is it a white car?

12. [ ] _____ Is it a gray car?

13. [ ] _____ Is it a black car?

| Chart 8 | **EXERCISE 75** |

┌───┐
│ AFFIRMATIVE   NEGATIVE   │
│   │
│ Yes, it is.   No, it isn't. It's _____ .   │
└───┘

Write the answer.

1. [1] Is the car red? *Yes, it is.* _____

2. [2] Is the car blue? *No, it isn't.   It's green.* _____

3. [4] Is the car yellow? _____

4. [11] Is the car brown? _____

5. [3] Is the car black? _____

6. [9] Is the car pink? _____

7. [7] Is the car green? _____

8. [10] Is the car orange? _____

9. [5] Is the car purple? _____

10. [8] Is the car white? _____

11. **6** Is the car gray? _____

12. **2** Is the car blue? _____

13. **1** Is the car red? _____

Chart 8 **EXERCISE 76**

```
┌──────┐
│  or  │
└──────┘
```

Write the question with or. *Then answer the question.*

1. **1** **2** *Is the car red or green?* _____

   2 *It's green.* _____

2. **5** **11** _____

   5 _____

3. **8** **3** _____

   3 _____

4. **9** **6** _____

   9 _____

5. **7** **10** _____

   7 _____

6. **11** **4** _____

   11 _____

7. **1** **6** _____

   6 _____

8. **1** **2** _____

   2 _____

EXERCISE 77

Write the question with or and the answer.

Chart 1   1. **6** **4**   *Is it a desk or a table?*
                    6   *It's a desk.*

          2. **7** **11** _____
                    11   _____

Chart 7   3. **7** **8**   *Is he happy or sad?*
                    7   *He's happy.*

          4. **17** **18** _____
                     17   _____

          5. **5** **6**   _____
                    6   _____

Chart 8   6. **8** **10** _____
                    8   _____

          7. **2** **3**   _____
                    2   _____

Write the statement. Use He's, She's, or It's.

Chart 7   8. **9**   *She's a thin woman.*

          9. **13** _____

          10. **11** _____

Chart 8   11. **7**   _____

          12. **6**   _____

          13. **1**   _____

Chart 14 | **EXERCISE 78**

Copy.

3 tie

$\underline{t}$ $\underline{i}$ $\underline{e}$

$\underline{tie}$

$\underline{tie}$

3 tie

— — —

——————

——————

4 jacket

— — — — — —

——————

——————

5 sweater

— — — — — —

——————

——————

6 shirt

— — — — —

——————

——————

8 suit

— — — —

——————

——————

9 coat

— — — —

——————

——————

10 dress

— — — — —

——————

——————

11 skirt

— — — — —

——————

——————

12 blouse

— — — — — —

——————

——————

→

13 purse

— — — — —

_____

_____

14 umbrella

— — — — — — —

_____

_____

15 hat

— — —

_____

_____

1 shoes

— — — — —

_____

_____

2 socks

— — — — —

_____

_____

7 pants

— — — — —

_____

_____

| Chart 7 | **EXERCISE 85** |

PRESENT PROGRESSIVE TENSE

STATEMENT | He's wearing a hat. | She's wearing socks.

/ | \   / | \

He is   She is

X   X

QUESTION | Is he wearing a hat? | Is she wearing socks?

SHORT ANSWERS

Yes, he is.   No, he isn't.

Yes, she is.   No, she isn't.

Write the question and the short answer.

1. **2** hat *Is he wearing a hat?*

     Yes, he is.

2. **14** socks *Is she wearing socks?*

     No, she isn't.

3. **13** shoes _____

_____

4. **10** hat _____

_____

5. **8** sweater _____

_____

→

6. **13** jacket _____

_____

7. **5** coat _____

_____

8. **12** suit _____

_____

9. **7** tie _____

_____

10. **16** shirt _____

_____

11. **6** socks _____

_____

12. **9** pants _____

_____

13. **14** socks _____

_____

14. **2** hat _____

_____

EXERCISE 89

Use Chart 4. Write the words.   He's wearing   He isn't wearing
                                     She's wearing   She isn't wearing

1. **7** *He's wearing* _____ a white shirt.

2. **2** _____ a blue hat.

3. **10** _____ black shoes.

4. **6** _____ a brown tie.

5. **3** _____ red pants.

6. **9** _____ an orange skirt.

7. **4** _____ a red skirt.

8. **1** _____ a gray dress.

9. **8** _____ a red dress.

10. **5** _____ a blue skirt.

Look at Chart 2. Write the question. Use What's.

11. **1** *What's he wearing?* _____

12. **10** _____

13. **11** _____

14. **15** _____

15. **2** _____

16. **1** _____

| Chart 16 | **EXERCISE 90** |

Copy.

1 behind

— — — — — — —

————————

————————

2 between

— — — — — — —

————————

————————

3 in front of

— — — — — — — — — —

————————————

————————————

4 next to

— — — — — —

————————

————————

5 in

— —

————

————

6 on

— — —

————

————

7 under

— — — — —

————————

————————

8 above

— — — — —

————————

————————

Chart 16 **EXERCISE 91**

Circle the correct spelling.

1. **1** (behind) behin
2. **7** undre under
3. **5** in ni
4. **4** next to nex to
5. **8** above abov
6. **2** betewen between
7. **3** in fron tof in front of
8. **6** on no

Chart 16 **EXERCISE 92**

Write the letters.

1. **1** behi *n d*
2. **6** _ n
3. **5** _ n
4. **7** u _ _ er
5. **3** in fro _ _ of
6. **8** ab _ ve
7. **4** n _ _ t to
8. **2** bet _ _ en

Chart 16 **EXERCISE 93**

Write the words. behind between in front of next to
in on under above

1. **1** The girl is *behind* the car.
2. **6** The girl is the car.
3. **3** The girl is the car.
4. **5** The girl is the car.
5. **2** The girl is the cars.
6. **8** The girl is the car.

→

7. **4** The girl is _____ the car.

8. **7** The girl is _____ the car.

| Chart 16 | **EXERCISE 94** |

Write the correct word.   is   isn't

1. **1** The girl _is_____ behind the car.

2. **1** The girl _____ behind the car.

3. **2** The girl _isn't_____ in front of the cars.

4. **2** The girl _____ in front of the cars.

5. **3** The girl _____ next to the car.

6. **4** The girl _____ next to the car.

7. **5** The girl _____ in the car.

8. **6** The girl _____ above the car.

9. **7** The girl _____ under the car.

10. **8** The girl _____ on the car.

11. **5** The girl _____ under the car.

12. **2** The girl _____ between the cars.

13. **8** The girl _____ in front of the car.

14. **3** The girl _____ above the car.

15. **6** The girl _____ on the car.

16. **7** The girl _____ next to the car.

17. **4** The girl _____ in front of the car.

It's Your Cue

What is on your desk or table? Write two statements.

_____

_____

| Chart 6 | **EXERCISE 101** |

Copy.

bus   chicken

— — —   — — — — — — —

_____   _____

_____   _____

chickens   mailbox

— — — — — — —   — — — — — — —

_____   _____

_____   _____

taxi   truck

— — — —   — — — — —

_____   _____

_____   _____

Copy the numbers.

one   two

— — —   — — —

_____   _____

_____   _____

$\longrightarrow$

three   four

_ _ _ _ _   _ _ _ _

_____   _____

_____   _____

five   six

_ _ _ _   _ _ _

_____   _____

_____   _____

seven   eight

_ _ _ _ _   _ _ _ _ _

_____   _____

_____   _____

Match the number with the word.

1 ——————————————   two

2   ————————→ one

3   seven

4   five

5   three

6   eight

7   four

8   six

Chart 6	**EXERCISE 102**

Write the words.   behind   between   in front of

next to   in   on

1. Four chickens are _behind_____ the waitress.

2. One chicken is _____ the table.

3. Eight chickens are _____ the workman.

4. Two chickens are _____ the old man and the little girl.

5. Two chickens are _____ the taxi.

6. Three chickens are _____ the photographer.

7. One chicken is _____ the dog.

8. Three chickens are _____ the truck.

9. One chicken is _____ the truck.

10. Five chickens are _____ the truck and the bus.

11. Seven chickens are _____ the bus.

12. One chicken is _____ the mailbox.

13. Six chickens are _____ the mailman.

14. Four chickens are _____ the waitress.

Chart 6 | **EXERCISE 103**

Fill in the chart below for "Downtown Accident."

What?	Where?
one chicken	*on the table*
	in front of the dog
two chickens	
three chickens	*in front of the photographer*
four chickens	
five chickens	
six chickens	
seven chickens	
eight chickens	

| Chart 6 | **EXERCISE 104** |

SINGULAR	One chicken **is** on the table.
There is	one chicken on the table.
PLURAL	Four chickens **are** behind the waitress.
There are four chickens	behind the waitress.

Circle the correct statement.

1.
There is one chicken is in front of the truck.

(There is one chicken in front of the truck.)

2.
Five chickens are between the truck and the bus.

Five chickens between the truck and the bus.

3.
There two chickens behind the old man and the little girl.

There are two chickens behind the old man and the little girl.

4.
Three chickens in front of the photographer.

Three chickens are in front of the photographer.

5.
There are four chickens behind the waitress.

There are four chickens are behind the waitress.

6.
One chicken on the table.

One chicken is on the table.

7.
There one chicken in front of the dog.

There is one chicken in front of the dog.

Chart 6 | **EXERCISE 105**

	SINGULAR	PLURAL
	One chicken is . . .	Three chickens are . . .
	There is one chicken . . .	There are three chickens . . .

Circle There is *or* There are. *Then write the statement with* There is *or* There are.

1. One chicken is on the table.

    (There is)
    There are   *There is one chicken on the table.*
    _____

2. Four chickens are behind the waitress.

    There is
    (There are)   *There are four chickens behind*
    the waitress.

3. Eight chickens are next to the workman.

    There is
    There are   _____
    _____

4. Two chickens are behind the old man and the little girl.

    There is
    There are   _____
    _____

5. Three chickens are in front of the photographer.

    There is
    There are   _____
    _____

6. One chicken is in front of the dog.

   There is
   There are _____

7. Five chickens are between the truck and the bus.

   There is
   There are _____

8. One chicken is in front of the truck.

   There is
   There are _____

9. Seven chickens are on the bus.

   There is
   There are _____

Chart 6 | **EXERCISE 106**

	QUESTION	ANSWER	
		AFFIRMATIVE	NEGATIVE
SINGULAR	Is there ...?	Yes, there is.	No, there is not. ↘↙ No, there isn't.
PLURAL	Are there ...?	Yes, there are.	No, there are not. ↘↙ No, there aren't.

Answer the question.

1. Are there five chickens on the truck?

   No, there aren't.   _There are three chickens._

2. Is there one chicken on the table?

   Yes, there is.

3. Is there one chicken between the truck and the bus?

   No, there isn't.   _There are five chickens._

4. Are there eight chickens next to the workman?

   _____

5. Are there three chickens in front of the photographer?

   _____

6. Are there two chickens in front of the dog?

   _____   _____

7. Are there seven chickens on the bus?

   _____

8. Is there one chicken behind the old man and the little girl?

   _____ _____

9. Are there five chickens behind the waitress?

   _____ _____

10. Is there one chicken in the mailbox?

    _____

11. Are there three chickens behind the taxi?

    _____ _____

12. Is there one chicken in front of the truck?

    _____

13. Are there seven chickens behind the mailman?

    _____ _____

It's Your Cue

Where are you? Write one statement. Use I'm.

_____

What is there in the room where you are? Write three statements.
Use There is *or* There are.

_____

_____

_____

Chart 6 **EXERCISE 107**

Write the words in the correct order to make a statement.

1. one   there   chicken   is   the   mailbox   in
   There is one chicken in the mailbox.

2. chickens   are   two   taxi   the   behind

   _____

3. there   eight   chickens   are   to   the   next   workman

   _____

   _____

4. seven   are   chickens   the   mailman   behind

   _____

5. is   one   chicken   of   in   the   truck   front

   _____

6. are   five   there   chickens   truck   between   the   the   bus   and

   _____

   _____

7. one   there   chicken   is   the   mailbox   in

   _____

EXERCISE 108

Write the correct words.

behind between in front of

is are

next to in on under above

Chart 6
1. There _____*is*_____ one chicken _____*in*_____ the mailbox.

2. There _____ three chickens _____ the truck.

3. There _____ two chickens _____ the taxi.

4. There _____ one chicken _____ the table.

Chart 11
5. There _____ a picture _____ the bed.

6. There _____ a radio _____ the table.

7. There _____ a chest _____ the bed.

8. There _____ a telephone _____ the lamp.

Chart 14
9. There _____*are*_____ shoes.

10. There _____ a suit.

11. There _____ an umbrella.

12. There _____ pants.

Chart 16
13. **5** There _____ a girl _____ the car.

14. **7** There _____ a girl _____ the car.

15. **4** There _____ a girl _____ the car.

16. **3** There _____ a girl _____ the car.

Chart 10 **READING TO WRITE 1**

The House

There are six people and a dog in this house. Upstairs, a girl is in the bathroom. She's taking a bath. A man is hanging up his suit in the bedroom.

Downstairs, an old man and a woman are in the living room. The old man is watching TV, and the woman is reading the newspaper. A boy is in the kitchen. He's playing the guitar. An old woman is on the back porch. She's opening the door. There's a dog downstairs too. It's sleeping on the rug in the hall.

A. *Answer the question with a complete statement.*

1. Where is the old man? *He's in the living room.*

2. What is the old man doing? *He's watching TV.*

3. What is the girl doing? _____

4. What is the man upstairs doing? _____

5. Where is the old woman? _____

6. Where is the woman? _____

7. Where is the boy? _____

8. What is the dog doing? _____

B. *These verbs are in the story "The House." Write the verbs with* -ing.

VERB	VERB + ing		VERB	VERB + ing
1. hang	_____		2. open	_____
3. play	_____		4. read	_____
5. sleep	_____		6. watch	_____
7. take	_____	tak¢		

C. Fill in the chart below for "The House."

	Who?	Doing What?

Upstairs
  bedroom
 	
  bathroom
	_____	*hanging up his suit* _____
		
		_____

Downstairs
  living room
 	
  kitchen
 	
  hall
 	
  back porch
	an old man ____
	_____
	
	_____
	
	a dog _____
	
	_____
		_____
		reading the newspaper ____
		
		_____
		
		_____
		
		_____

D. **It's Your Cue**

Use the above chart. Write about upstairs in "The House."
Who is upstairs? What are the people doing upstairs?

_____

_____

_____

_____

$\longrightarrow$

E. *Write the words in the correct order to make a statement.*

1. people   six   there   are   house   in   this

   <u>*There are six people in this house.*</u>

2. a   boy   the   is   kitchen   in

   _____

3. door   the   she's   opening

   _____

4. man   a   is   suit   up   his   hanging

   _____

5. sleeping   on   it's   rug   the   hall   in   the

   _____

6. woman   an   old   the   on   porch   is   back

   _____

7. girl   a   the   is   bathroom   in

   _____

8. downstairs   a   there's   dog

   _____

9. old   the   man   TV   is   watching

   _____

10. playing   the   he's   guitar

   _____

F. *This story is from Chart 10. Write a correct word in each blank.*

The House

There are six people and a dog in this house.

Upstairs, _____*a*_____ girl is in the bathroom.
               1

_____ taking a bath. A man _____
      2   3

hanging up his suit in _____ bedroom.
                              4

Downstairs, an old man _____ a woman
                               5

are in the _____ room. The old man is
                6

_____ TV, and the woman is _____
      7   8

the newspaper. A boy is _____ the kitchen. He's
                             9

playing the _____ . An old woman is on
                  10

_____ back porch. She's opening the _____ .
      11   12

There's a dog downstairs too. _____ sleeping
                                      13

on the rug in _____ hall.
                    14

Chart 3 | **EXERCISE 109**

Copy.

1 train station

_ _ _ _ _

_ _ _ _ _ _ _

———————————

———————————

2 airport

_ _ _ _ _ _

———————————

———————————

3 hospital

_ _ _ _ _ _ _

———————————

———————————

4 museum

_ _ _ _ _

———————————

———————————

5 post office

_ _ _ _   _ _ _ _ _

———————————

———————————

6 movie theater

_ _ _ _ _

_ _ _ _ _ _

———————————

———————————

7 bank

_ _ _ _

———————

———————

8 garage

_ _ _ _ _

———————

———————

9 bus station

_ _ _   _ _ _ _ _

———————————

———————————

10 drugstore

_ _ _ _ _ _ _ _

———————————

———————————

11 bookstore

_ _ _ _ _ _ _ _ _

_____

_____

12 restaurant

_ _ _ _ _ _ _ _ _

_____

_____

13 train

_ _ _ _ _

_____

_____

14 plane

_ _ _ _

____

____

15 taxi

_ _ _ _

____

____

16 motorcycle

_ _ _ _ _ _ _ _ _ _

_____

_____

17 car

_ _ _

___

___

18 truck

_ _ _ _ _

_____

_____

19 bus

_ _ _

___

___

20 bike

_ _ _ _

____

____

Chart 3 | **EXERCISE 110**

Circle the correct spelling.

1. **1** (train station) train statoin
2. **7** ban bank
3. **10** drugstore durgstore
4. **2** airport airprot
5. **8** garge garage
6. **17** rac car
7. **13** trian train
8. **4** museum muesum
9. **9** bus tation bus station
10. **14** plan plane
11. **3** hospital hopsital
12. **18** turck truck
13. **12** restaurant restarant
14. **6** movie theater movie thetaer
15. **20** bik bike
16. **15** txai taxi
17. **5** post office post ofice
18. **19** bus sub
19. **11** bookstor bookstore
20. **16** motocycle motorcycle
21. **1** train station train statoin

Chart 3 | **EXERCISE 111**

Write the letters.

1. **1** tr _a_ _i_ n stat _i_ _o_ n
2. **2** _ _ rport
3. **3** ho _ _ ital
4. **4** mus _ _ m
5. **7** ba _ _
6. **10** _ _ ugstore
7. **18** tru _ _
8. **9** bus _ _ ation
9. **13** tr _ _ n
10. **12** rest _ _ rant
11. **20** b _ ke
12. **5** post off _ _ _
13. **19** b _ s
14. **17** ca _

| Chart 12 | **EXERCISE 117** |

Copy.

1 hamburger

_ _ _ _ _ _ _ _ _

_____

_____

2 hot dog

_ _ _   _ _ _

_____

_____

3 soup

_ _ _ _

_____

_____

4 salad

_ _ _ _ _

_____

_____

5 milk

_ _ _ _

_____

_____

6 ice cream

_ _ _   _ _ _ _ _

_____

_____

7 steak

_ _ _ _ _

_____

_____

8 fish

_ _ _ _

_____

_____

9 chicken

_ _ _ _ _ _ _

_____

_____

10 roll

_ _ _ _

_____

_____

$\longrightarrow$

11 sandwich

_ _ _ _ _ _ _ _

_____

_____

Chart 12 **EXERCISE 118**

Circle the correct spelling.

1. **1** hambruger (hamburger)   2. **9** chicken   chiken

3. **5** mik   milk   4. **8** fihs   fish

5. **4** sald   salad   6. **3** suop   soup

7. **7** staek   steak   8. **2** hot dog   hotdog

9. **11** sandwich   sanwich   10. **6** ice craem   ice cream

11. **10** rol   roll   12. **1** hambruger   hamburger

Chart 12 **EXERCISE 119**

Write the letters.

1. **1** hamb _u_ _r_ ger   2. **3** s _ _ p

3. **7** st _ _ k   4. **10** ro _ _

5. **6** ice cr _ _ m   6. **2** h _ t d _ g

7. **9** chi _ _ en   8. **5** mi _ k

9. **8** fi _ _   10. **4** sal _ d

11. **11** sandwi _ _   12. **1** hamb _ _ ger

Chart 12 | **EXERCISE 120**

Write the words.

COUNT NOUNS

	SINGULAR	PLURAL

1. `1` *a hamburger*   *hamburgers*

2. `7` _____   _____

3. `11` _____   _____ -ch + es

4. `2` _____   _____

5. `10` _____   _____

6. `1` _____   _____

MASS NOUNS

7. `3` *soup* _____

8. `5` _____

9. `8` _____

10. `6` _____

11. `4` _____

12. `9` _____

13. `3` _____

Chart 12 | **EXERCISE 121**

Copy.

eating   drinking

— — — — — — —   — — — — — — — —

_____   _____

_____   _____

I'm   You're   He's   She's

Write the statement.

1. **1** He *He's eating a hamburger.*

2. **3** She *She's eating soup.*

3. **10** I _____

4. **6** You _____

5. **5** She _____

6. **9** He _____

7. **2** You _____

8. **4** She _____

9. **8** He _____

10. **7** I _____

11. **11** You _____

12. **3** She _____

13. **1** He _____

11 cherry

— — — — — —

_____

_____

12 green bean

— — — — —   — — — —

_____

_____

13 tomato

— — — — — —

_____

_____

14 lettuce

— — — — — — —

_____

_____

15 pineapple

— — — — — — — — —

_____

_____

16 apple

— — — — —

_____

_____

17 potato

— — — — — —

_____

_____

Chart 13	**EXERCISE 125**

Circle the correct spelling.

1. **1** (pear)   paer   2. **9** pea   aep
3. **16** appel   apple   4. **5** grape   graep
5. **13** tomato tamato   6. **6** bannana   banana
7. **17** patato potato   8. **4** lenom   lemon

→

9. **3** orange oragne   10. **14** letuce lettuce

11. **15** pinapple pineapple   12. **11** chery cherry

13. **2** pech peach   14. **7** corn cron

15. **10** onoin onion   16. **8** carot carrot

17. **12** green been green bean   18. **1** pear paer

Chart 13	**EXERCISE 126**

Write the letters.

1. **1** p _e_ _a_ r   2. **10** o _ _ on

3. **8** carr _ t   4. **15** pin _ _ pple

5. **14** lettu _ _   6. **4** lem _ n

7. **3** ora _ _ e   8. **17** p _ tato

9. **11** cher _ _   10. **9** p _ a

11. **6** b _ n _ na   12. **2** p _ _ ch

13. **7** c _ _ n   14. **13** t _ mato

15. **16** ap _ _ e   16. **5** gr _ p _

17. **12** gre _ n b _ _ n   18. **1** p _ _ r

5. **9** we _____

6. **16** he _____

7. **17** you _____

8. **2** she _____

9. **15** we _____

10. **11** they _____

11. **13** they _____

12. **5** she _____

13. **6** you _____

14. **14** he _____

15. **10** we _____

16. **8** we _____

17. **4** they _____

18. **7** you _____

19. **1** he _____

Chart 5 | **EXERCISE 129**

Copy.

want   wants

— — — —   — — — — —

_____   _____

_____   _____

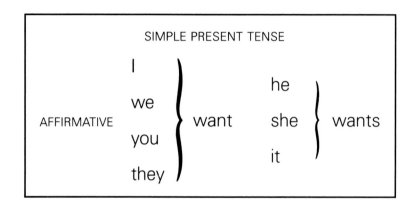

Write the subject pronoun with want *or* wants.

1. **1** *I want* _____

2. **7** *she wants* _____

3. **5** _____

4. **2** _____

5. **6** _____

6. **3** _____

7. **4** _____

8. **1** _____

9. **7** _____

Chart 13 | **EXERCISE 130**

Copy.

some

— — — — —

——————

——————

AFFIRMATIVE	He wants some green beans. He wants some lettuce.
	He wants **some** green beans **and** lettuce.

want	some . . . and
wants	

Write the affirmative statement.

1. **12** **14** He *He wants some green beans and lettuce.*

2. **1** I *I want some pears.*

3. **14** She *She wants some lettuce.*

4. **6** **11** We _____

5. **3** She _____

6. **4** **15** He _____

7. **17** They _____

8. **2** **8** I _____

9. **7** **10** She _____

→

10. **9** They _____

11. **13** He _____

12. **5** **16** I _____

| Chart 5 | **EXERCISE 131**

Copy.

don't want   doesn't want

_ _ _ _ _   _ _ _ _ _   _ _ _ _ _ _ _   _ _ _ _ _

_____   _____

_____   _____

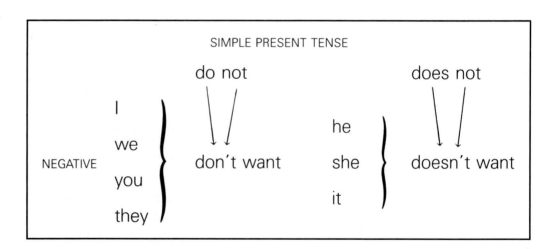

Write the subject pronoun with don't want *or* doesn't want.

1. **1** *I don't want* _____

2. **7** *she doesn't want* _____

3. **4** _____

4. **6** _____

5. **2** _____

6. **3** _____

7. **5** _____

8. **1** _____

9. **7** _____

| Chart 13 | **EXERCISE 132** |

Copy.

any

— — —

_____

_____

| NEGATIVE | He doesn't want any cherries.   He doesn't want any lettuce. |
| | He doesn't want **any** cherries **or** lettuce. |

| don't want |
| doesn't want |

| any . . . or |

Write the negative statement.

1. **11** **14** He *He doesn't want any cherries or lettuce.* _____

2. **1** She *She doesn't want any pears.* _____

3. **7** They *They don't want any corn.* _____

4. **4** I _____

$\longrightarrow$

5. **2** **17** We _____

6. **5** They _____

7. **3** **13** I _____

8. **6** She _____

9. **9** **16** They _____

10. **8** We _____

11. **7** **10** He _____

12. **15** I _____

13. **1** She _____

14. **7** They _____

15. **11** **14** He _____

Chart 13	**EXERCISE 133**

AFFIRMATIVE	NEGATIVE
some	any

Write the picture number. Then write some *or* any.

1. *1* We want _____*some*_____ pears.

2. *8* They don't want _____*any*_____ carrots.

3. ☐ I want _____ bananas.

4. ☐ We want _____ cherries.

5. ☐ You want _____ peaches.

6. ☐ I don't want _____ apples.

7. [ ] He doesn't want _____ green beans.

8. [ ] She wants _____ corn.

9. [ ] She doesn't want _____ potatoes.

10. [ ] I want _____ lemons.

11. [ ] He wants _____ lettuce.

12. [ ] They want _____ oranges.

13. [ ] We don't want _____ onions.

14. [ ] He doesn't want _____ tomatoes.

15. [ ] I don't want _____ grapes.

16. [ ] They want _____ pineapples.

17. [ ] They don't want _____ peas.

| Chart 13 | **EXERCISE 134** |

AFFIRMATIVE	NEGATIVE
some . . . and	any . . . or

Write the picture number. Then circle the correct words.

1. [1][16] We want （some pears and apples.）
   any pears or apples.

2. [2][9] They don't want
   some peaches and peas.
   （any peaches or peas.）

3. [ ][ ] He wants
   any cherries and lettuce.
   some cherries and lettuce.

→

4. ☐ ☐ She doesn't want   any oranges or pineapples.
                                                   some oranges and pineapples.

5. ☐ ☐ I want   any onions or potatoes.
                                some onions and potatoes.

6. ☐ ☐ You don't want   some grapes and lemons.
                                          any grapes or lemons.

7. ☐ ☐ I don't want   some bananas and green beans.
                                    any bananas or green beans.

8. ☐ ☐ They want   some potatoes and corn.
                                any potatoes and corn.

9. ☐ ☐ We want   some carrots and tomatoes.
                              any carrots and tomatoes.

| Chart 12 | **EXERCISE 135** |

AFFIRMATIVE   NEGATIVE

some . . . and   any . . . or

Write the statement.

1. **4** **8** I (NEGATIVE) *I don't want any salad or fish.*

2. **3** **10** He (NEGATIVE) *He doesn't want any soup or rolls.*

3. **5** **11** We (AFFIRMATIVE) *We want some milk and sandwiches.*

4. **1** **6** She (AFFIRMATIVE) _____

_____

5. **3** **9** They (AFFIRMATIVE) _____

_____

6. **2** **5** You (NEGATIVE) _____

_____

7. **4** **10** I (NEGATIVE) _____

_____

8. **8** **10** She (NEGATIVE) _____

_____

9. **3** **11** We (AFFIRMATIVE) _____

_____

$\longrightarrow$

10. **1** **2** They (NEGATIVE) _____

_____

11. **4** **8** I (NEGATIVE) _____

_____

12. **3** **10** He (NEGATIVE) _____

_____

13. **5** **11** We (AFFIRMATIVE) _____

_____

B. *These verbs are from the story "The Party." Write the verbs with* -ing.

	VERB	VERB + ing		VERB	VERB + ing
1.	eat	_____	2.	hold	_____
3.	play	_____	4.	sing	_____
5.	stand	_____	6.	talk	_____
7.	dance	_____ danc¢	8.	give	_____ giv¢
9.	have	_____ hav¢	10.	run	_____ runn
11.	sit	_____ sitt			

C. *Fill in the chart below for "The Party."*

Who?	Doing what?
many people	*talking*
_____	*sitting at the yellow table*
_____	*dancing*
_____	*eating*
_____	*playing the guitar*
people on the blankets	_____
some children	_____
other children	_____
_____	*giving milk to the kittens*
three women	_____
_____	*having fun*

→

D. **It's Your Cue**

IMAGINE . . . you are at the party. What are you doing?
Write three statements.

_____

_____

_____

E. Write the words in the correct order to make a statement.

1. summer   it's

   It's summer. _____

2. a   there   is   party   the   backyard   in

   _____

3. playing   a   woman   guitar   is   the   tree   a   under

   _____

   _____

4. people   some   eating   are

   _____

5. blanket   the   people   the   on   singing   are

   _____

   _____

6. three   dancing   are   couples

   _____

7. talking   people   are   many

   _____

8. fun   everyone   having   is   party   at   the

_____

9. is   food   of   a   there   lot   the   table   on

_____

F. This story is from Chart 15. Write a correct word in each blank.

The Party

It's summer. There is a party in _____*the*_____ backyard.
                                        1

Many people are _____. Some people are eating.
                      2

Two _____ are sitting at the yellow _____.
        3   4

Three couples are dancing. A _____ is playing
                                    5

the guitar under _____ tree. The people on the
                        6

blankets _____ singing.
              7

Some children are running, _____ other children
                                  8

are playing with _____ puppies. A boy is giving
                        9

_____ to the kittens.
      10

There is _____ lot of food on the _____.
              11   12

Three women are standing and _____ . Two of the
                                    13

women are holding more _____. Everyone is having
                              14

fun at _____ party.
            15

Chart 17 | **EXERCISE 137**

Copy.

1 play soccer

_ _ _ _   _ _ _ _ _ _

_____

_____

2 play tennis

_ _ _ _   _ _ _ _ _ _

_____

_____

3 play volleyball

_ _ _ _   _ _ _ _ _ _ _ _ _

_____

_____

4 play baseball

_ _ _ _   _ _ _ _ _ _ _

_____

_____

5 play chess

_ _ _ _   _ _ _ _ _

_____

_____

6 play basketball

_ _ _ _   _ _ _ _ _ _ _ _ _ _

_____

_____

7 play cards

_ _ _ _   _ _ _ _ _

_____

_____

8 play golf

_ _ _ _   _ _ _ _

_____

_____

9 ski

_ _ _

_____

_____

10 swim

_ _ _ _

_____

_____

11 skate

_ _ _ _ _

_____

_____

12 sail

_ _ _ _

_____

_____

Chart 17 | **EXERCISE 138**

Circle the correct spelling.

1. **1**   play socer   (play soccer)
2. **4**   play baseball   play basball
3. **9**   iks   ski
4. **12**   sail   sial
5. **2**   play tennis   play tenis
6. **7**   play crads   play cards
7. **6**   play baksetball   play basketball
8. **3**   play volleyball   play voleyball
9. **8**   play glof   play golf
10. **5**   play ches   play chess
11. **11**   skat   skate
12. **10**   swim   siwm
13. **1**   play socer   play soccer

Chart 17 | **EXERCISE 139**

Write the letters.

1. **5**   play ch _e_ ss   2. **9**   sk __
3. **6**   play bask __ tball   4. **1**   play socc __ r
5. **10**   __ __ im   6. **3**   play voll __ __ ball
7. **12**   s __ __ l   8. **2**   play tenn __ s
9. **7**   play ca __ __ s   10. **11**   sk __ t __
11. **4**   play b __ s __ ball   12. **8**   play go __ __
13. **5**   play ch __ ss

13. ▢ Do you 🧍 play baseball?

Yes _____

14. ▢ Does he play soccer?

Yes _____

15. ▢ Do you 👥 ski?

No _____

Chart 12 **EXERCISE 143**

Write the picture number. Then write the word.

　　　Do　　　don't　　　want

　　　Does　　　doesn't　　　wants

1. ▢ *1* _____*Does*_____ she want a hamburger?

Yes, she _____*wants*_____ a hamburger.

2. ▢ Do you _____ a hot dog?

No, I _____ want a hot dog.

3. ▢ _____ he want fish?

Yes, he _____ fish.

4. ▢ Do you _____ a roll?

No, I _____ want a roll.

→

5. [ ] _____ you want milk?

Yes, we _____ milk.

6. [ ] Does she _____ soup?

No, she _____ want any soup.

7. [ ] _____ he want a sandwich?

No, he _____ want a sandwich.

8. [ ] _____ they want salad?

No, they _____ want any salad.

9. [ ] Do you _____ chicken?

Yes, I _____ chicken.

10. [ ] _____ he want ice cream?

Yes, he _____ ice cream.

11. [ ] Do they _____ steaks?

No, they _____ want any steaks.

12. [ ] _____ she want a hamburger?

Yes, she _____ a hamburger.

Chart 12 | **EXERCISE 144**

COUNT NOUNS	MASS NOUNS		do
How many . . . ?	How much . . . ?		does

Write the question with How much *or* How many.

1. **1** you *How many hamburgers do you want?*

2. **9** he *How much chicken does he want?*

3. **7** they _____

4. **2** she _____

5. **10** they _____

6. **6** he _____

7. **3** you _____

8. **4** she _____

9. **11** they _____

10. **5** you _____

11. **8** he _____

12. **9** he _____

13. **1** you _____

Chart 13 | **EXERCISE 145**

	COUNT NOUNS	MASS NOUNS
QUESTION	How many . . . ?	How much . . . ?
AFFIRMATIVE ANSWER	a lot of	a lot of
NEGATIVE ANSWER	not . . . many	not . . . much

do	don't
does	doesn't

much
many
a lot of

Write the question. Then write the affirmative or negative answer.

1. **1** you _How many pears do you want?_

   (AFFIRMATIVE) _I want a lot of pears._

2. **14** he _How much lettuce does he want?_

   (NEGATIVE) _He doesn't want much lettuce._

3. **11** they _How many cherries do they want?_

   (NEGATIVE) _They don't want many cherries._

4. **5** she _____

   (AFFIRMATIVE) _____

5. **8** you _____

   (AFFIRMATIVE) _____

6. **7** you _____

   (NEGATIVE) _____

7. **10** they _____

      (AFFIRMATIVE) _____

8. **13** she _____

      (NEGATIVE) _____

9. **17** he _____

      (AFFIRMATIVE) _____

10. **14** they _____

      (NEGATIVE) _____

11. **11** they _____

      (NEGATIVE) _____

12. **1** you _____

      (AFFIRMATIVE) _____

13. **14** he _____

      (NEGATIVE) _____

EXERCISE 146

Use Chart 17. Write the question and the short answer.

1. **10** you   _Do you swim?_

   No _No, I don't._

2. **4** he _____

   Yes _____

3. **1** they _____

   Yes _____

4. **7** she _____

   No _____

5. **6** you _____

   Yes _____

6. **11** you _____

   No _____

Write the question. Use How much *or* How many.

Chart 12   7. **6** you _How much ice cream do you want?_

8. **11** he _____

Chart 13   9. **10** you _____

10. **5** they _____

11. **14** she _____

Chart 18 **READING TO WRITE 4**

Outside the Hotel

The big hotel is next to the ocean. Many people are staying there. They are all on vacation.

Some people are playing together. They are playing soccer, baseball, volleyball, and tennis. Other people are sitting at tables or relaxing on the hotel porch. Some people are swimming.

A man is fishing in the ocean, and a woman is riding a horse. A family is riding in the car. Everyone is having fun on vacation.

A. Answer the question with a complete statement.

1. What is next to the ocean?

   The big hotel is next to the ocean.

2. Who is fishing in the ocean?

   _____

3. What are some people playing?

   _____

4. What is a woman riding?

   _____

5. Who is riding in the car?

   _____

6. Where are some people relaxing?

   _____

7. Where are some people sitting?

   _____

→

B. These verbs are from the story "Outside the Hotel." Write the verbs with -ing.

	VERB	VERB + ing		VERB	VERB + ing
1.	fish	_____	2.	play	_____
3.	relax	_____	4.	stay	_____
5.	have	_____havɇ	6.	ride	_____ridɇ
7.	sit	_____sitt	8.	swim	_____swimm

C. Fill in the chart below for "Outside the Hotel."

How many people?	Doing what?
4	playing tennis
_____	sitting at tables
_____	swimming
_____	riding a horse
_____	playing soccer
_____	playing volleyball
_____	riding in the car
_____	fishing
_____	playing baseball
_____	relaxing on the hotel porch

D. **It's Your Cue**

IMAGINE you are at the hotel on vacation. What are you doing? Write three statements.

_____

_____

_____

EXERCISE 153

Use Chart 17. Write the picture number. Then write the word.

Do   don't   like

Does   doesn't   likes

1. [/] I _____*don't*_____ like to play soccer.

2. [   ] _____ she like to skate?

3. [   ] He _____ to play baseball.

4. [   ] _____ they like to play basketball?

5. [   ] He _____ like to ski.

6. [   ] _____ you like to play tennis?

7. [   ] We _____ like to play chess.

8. [   ] She _____ to swim.

9. [   ] _____ he like to play tennis?

10. [   ] She _____ like to play golf.

11. [   ] We _____ to sail.

12. [   ] They _____ to play cards.

| Chart 19 | **READING TO WRITE 5** |

The Seasons

1   It's a spring day. In the spring, the weather is warm or cool. Today it's raining. Many pretty flowers are growing. The woman is carrying an umbrella. The boy is walking in a puddle. He's wearing a yellow raincoat. The dog is following the boy.

2   It's a summer day. In the summer, the weather is hot. This family is at the beach. The father is reading the newspaper. The mother is lying in the sun. The children are playing. They are all wearing swimsuits.

3   It's a fall day. In the fall, the weather is cool or warm. It's windy in the fall too. This woman is raking leaves. The boy is helping her. He's carrying a basket of leaves. She's wearing a scarf, and he's wearing a cap.

4   It's a winter day. In the winter, the weather is cold. Today it's snowing. People are walking outside. They are all wearing warm clothes. One woman is walking a dog. It's wearing a sweater.

5   It's morning. The sun is rising.

6   It's afternoon. The sun is shining.

7   It's night. The moon and the stars are shining.

A. Answer the question with a complete statement.

1 1. What season is it?

_____

2. Is it raining today?

_____

3. What is the woman carrying?

_____

2 4. What season is it?

_____

5. Is it cool or hot?

_____

6. What are they all wearing?

_____

3 7. What season is it?

_____

8. What is the boy carrying?

_____

4 9. What season is it?

_____

10. Is it raining?

_____

11. What are people wearing?

_____

$\longrightarrow$

12. What is the dog wearing?

_____

5 13. What is the sun doing?

_____

6 14. What is the sun doing?

_____

7 15. What time of day is it?

_____

B. *These verbs are in the story "The Seasons." Write the verbs with* -ing.

VERB   VERB + ing

1. carry   _____

2. follow _____

3. grow   _____

4. help   _____

5. play   _____

6. rain   _____

7. read   _____

8. snow   _____

9. walk   _____

10. wear   _____

11. rake   _____rak$\not{e}$

12. rise   _____ris$\not{e}$

13. shine _____shin$\not{e}$

14. lie   _____ly

F. This story is from Chart 20. Write a correct word in each blank.

In the Hotel

1   There are four people in the kitchen. The first cook is

baking _____*a*_____ ham, and the second cook
            1

_____ slicing a ham. The third _____ is
        2   3

making some soup. The _____ is making some
                            4

salad. A _____ is entering the kitchen too.
            5

_____ carrying a tray of dirty _____ .
        6   7

2   The guests are eating dinner in the dining room. Two

waitresses are waiting on _____ , and a waiter is
                                8

carrying _____ tray of food.
            9

3   A man and a woman are in their hotel room. They are

unpacking _____ suitcases.
                10

4   Some hotel guests are in the lounge. Four people are

playing cards. _____ woman is reading a book.
                    11

_____ tennis players are talking.
        12

The Alphabet

Aa Bb Cc Dd Ee Ff

Gg Hh Ii Jj Kk Ll

Mm Nn Oo Pp Qq Rr

Ss Tt Uu Vv Ww Xx

Yy Zz

1	2	3	4	5	6	7	8	9	10
11	12	13	14	15	16	17	18	19	20
21	22	23	24	25	26	27	28	29	30
31	32	33	34	35	36	37	38	39	40
41	42	43	44	45	46	47	48	49	50
51	52	53	54	55	56	57	58	59	60
61	62	63	64	65	66	67	68	69	70
71	72	73	74	75	76	77	78	79	80
81	82	83	84	85	86	87	88	89	90
91	92	93	94	95	96	97	98	99	100

STUDENT PROGRESS CHART FOR _____

EXERCISE NUMBER	DATE COMPLETED	CHECKED BY	COMMENTS